THE AMAZING SPIDER-MAN
JUMBO
COLORING & ACTIVITY BOOK

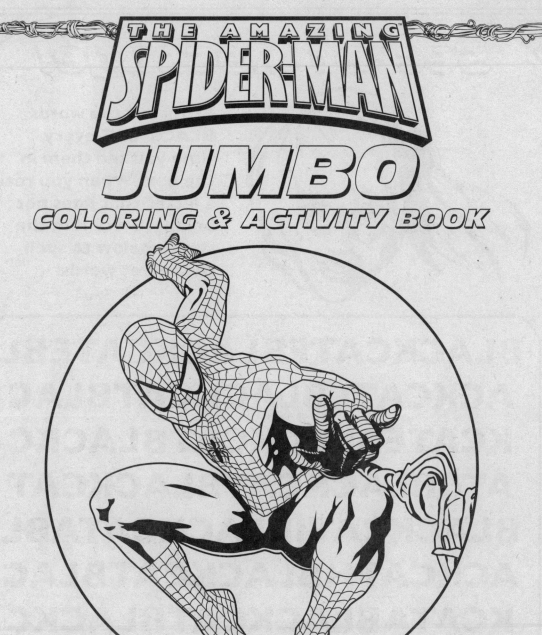

BENDON Publishing Int'l., Inc.
Ashland, OH 44805
www.bendonpub.com

Secret Message!

Cross out the words **BLACK CAT** every time you see them in the box. When you reach a letter that does not belong, write it in the circles below to spell the secret words!

BLACKCATFBLACKCATEBL
ACKCATLBLACKCATBLAC
KCATEBLACKCATBLACKC
ATCBLACKCATBLACKCAT
BLACKCATIBLACKCATABL
ACKCATHBLACKCATBLAC
KCATABLACKCATBLACKC
ATRBLACKCATBLACKCAT
DBLACKCATBLACKCATY

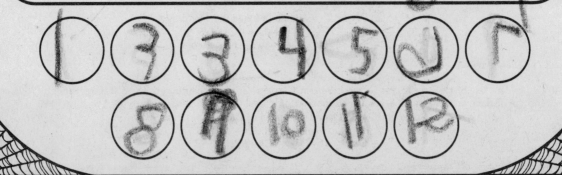

Cross Patch!

Using the words from the list, complete the cross patch puzzle.

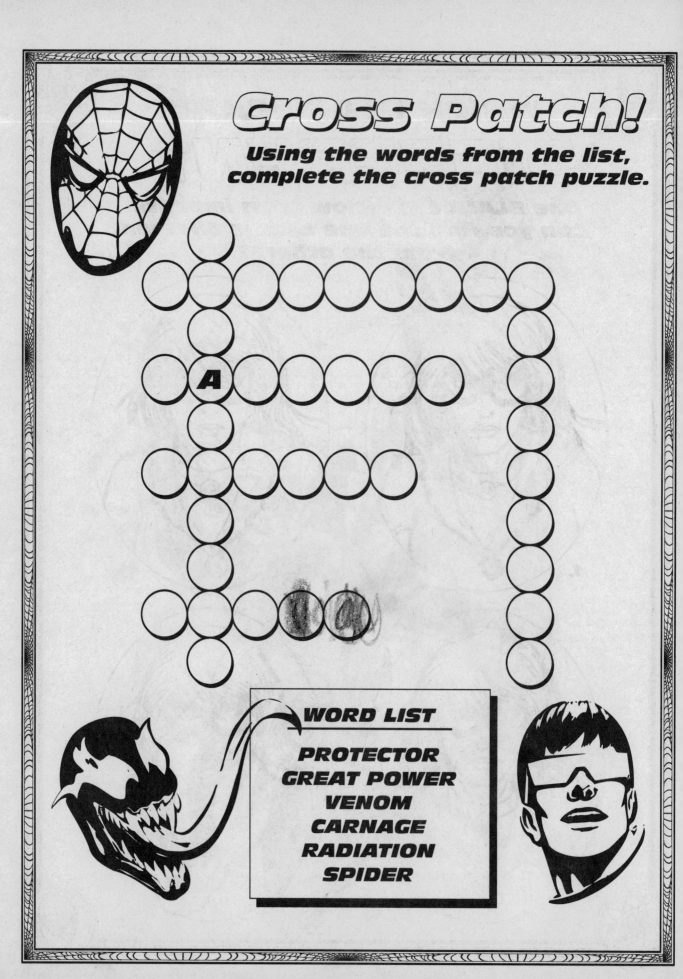

WORD LIST

PROTECTOR
GREAT POWER
VENOM
CARNAGE
RADIATION
SPIDER

WHICH BLACK CAT IS
DIFFERENT?

One BLACK CAT below is an imposter. Can you find the one that is different from the others?

1.

2.

3.

4.

Which 2 are EXACTLY the SAME?

Look at the four pictures. Two of them are exactly alike. Can you find them?

1.

2.

3.

4.

Answers: Numbers 2 and 4.

Finish the Picture!
Finish drawing the Black Cat!

Draw
SPIDER-MAN

Using the grid as a guide, draw a picture of Spider-man in the box below.

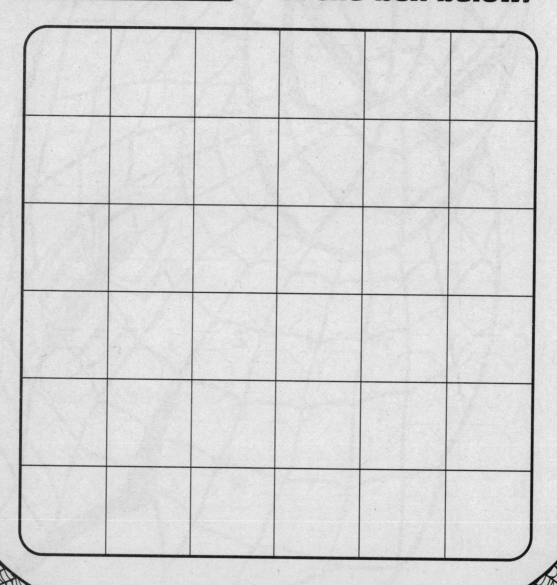

Follow the Path

Using the letters in order from the word

LIZARD

follow the correct path to find your way through the maze!

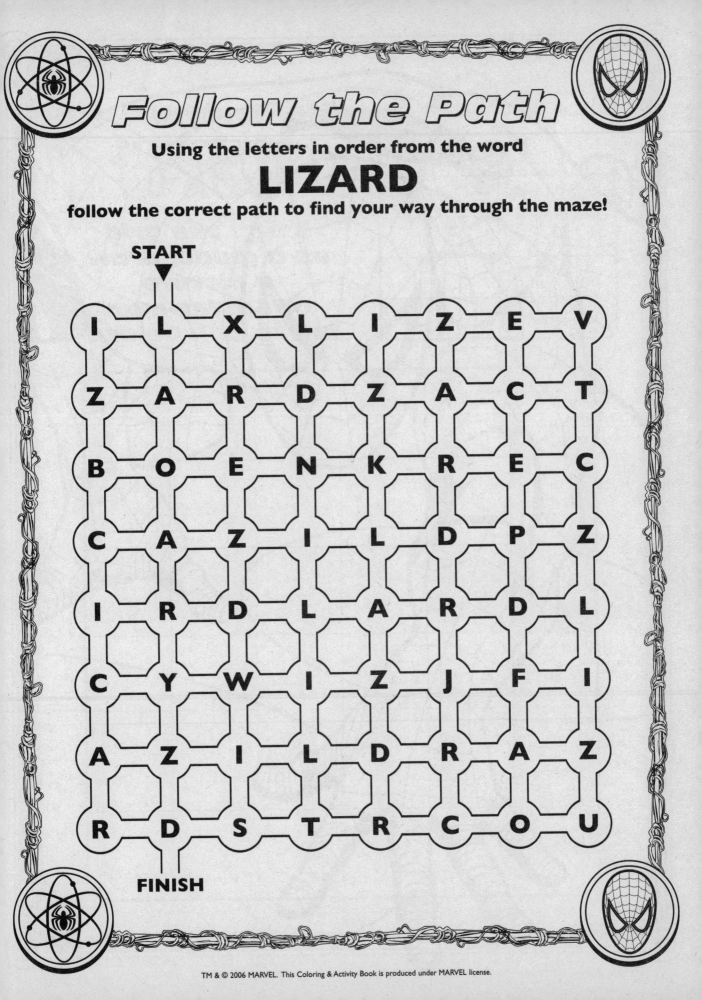

START

FINISH

WHICH WAY?

Help Spider-Man find his way through the maze to capture Electro!

START

FINISH

Word Scramble

Using the words from the list, unscramble the letters to correctly spell the names and words!

NOEMV _____

ECTTOOPRR _____

NARGAEC _____

ATIIDOANR _____

ZIANGMA _____

TULREVU _____

WORD LIST

AMAZING	CARNAGE
RADIATION	VENOM
PROTECTOR	VULTURE

BLACK CAT SQUARES

Taking turns, connect a line from one cat to another. Whoever makes the line that completes a box puts their initials inside the box. The person with the most squares at the end of the game wins!

EXAMPLE:

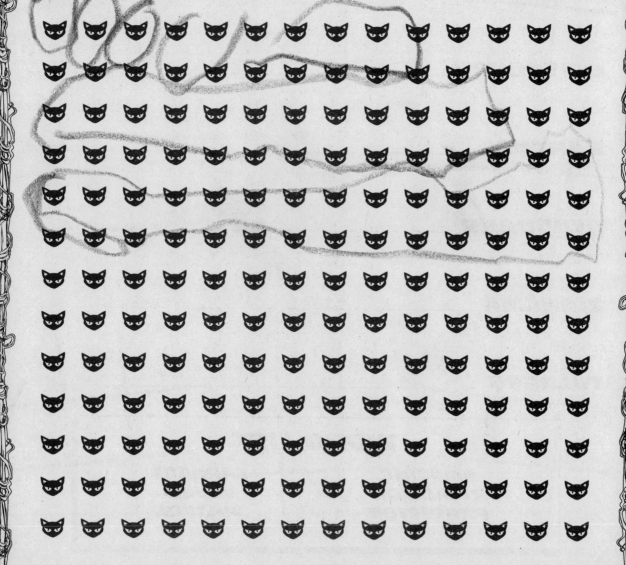

TIC-TAC-TOE

USE THESE SPACES TO CHALLENGE YOUR FAMILY AND FRIENDS!

DOCTOR OCTOPUS PUZZLE

Have a parent or care-giver cut out the puzzle pieces on the dotted lines.

Mix up the pieces, and put the picture back together!

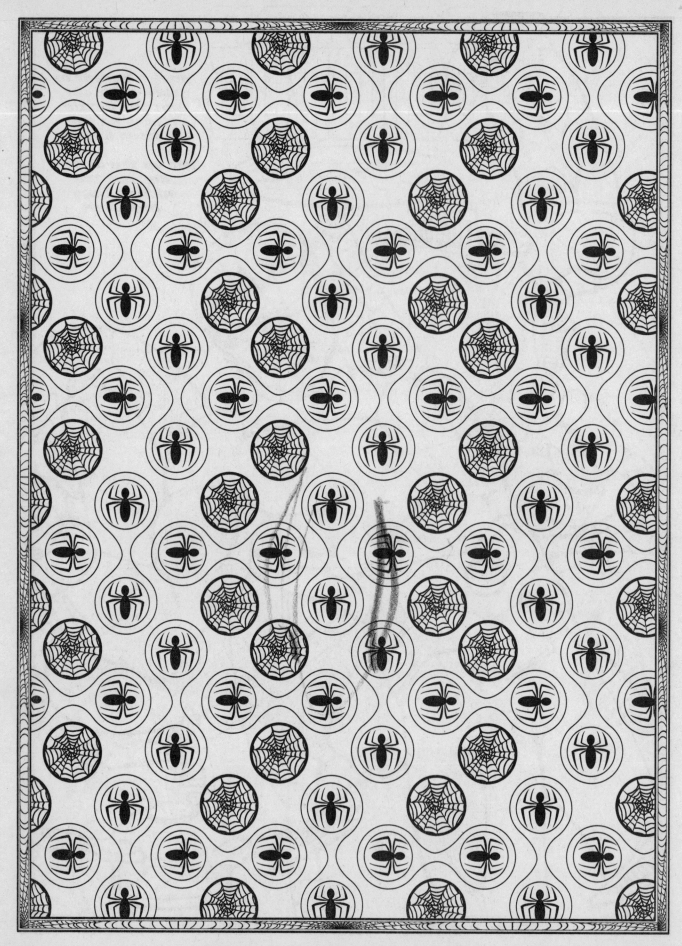

THE AMAZING SPIDER-MAN

WHICH ELECTRO IS
DIFFERENT?

**One ELECTRO below is an imposter.
Can you find the one that is different
from the others?**

1.

2.

3.

4.

TIC-TAC-TOE

USE THESE SPACES TO CHALLENGE YOUR FAMILY AND FRIENDS!

SPIDEY MAZE

Help the Amazing Spider-Man get through the maze and capture Doctor Octopus!

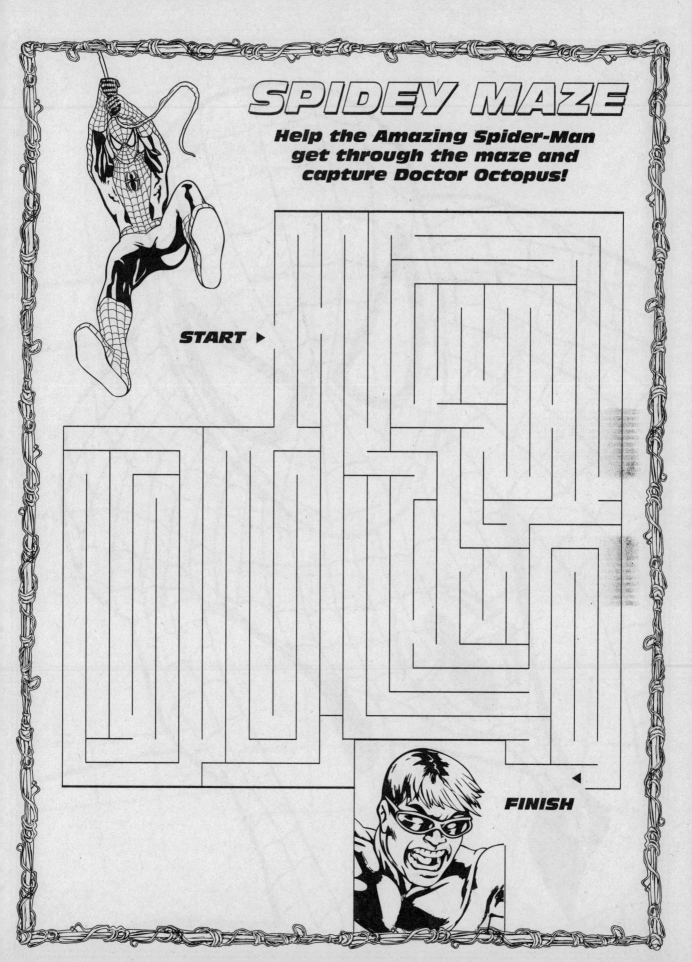

START ▶

FINISH ◀

Finish the Picture!

Where is Spider-Man? Draw your own exciting background to find out!

Which Piece is
MISSING?

Only one of the puzzle pieces below will fit. Can you find the missing piece and complete the puzzle?

A.

B.

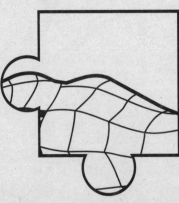

C.

WHO is WHO?

Only one set of letters can be used to spell the villains names correctly. Put a check next to the right one!

1.  RHINO

   A  NIHRR **B** ◯ ORNHI **C** ◯ ORNHH

2.  SANDMAN

   A ◯ NSSAMDN **B** ◯ DMNASNN

   C ◯ MDANANS

3.  VENOM

   A ◯ NOEMV **B** ◯ MEVMO **C** ◯ EOMVM

4.  LIZARD

   A ◯ DEAZIL **B** ◯ ILAZDR **C** ◯ REZDIL

FIND THE WORDS

```
A  S  G  G  N  I  D  L  I  U  B
C  W  H  Q  W  K  R  S  T  Y  P
R  I  C  V  E  C  S  G  N  M  N
C  N  S  R  N  H  H  A  X  A  P
O  G  I  T  I  W  S  O  M  R  M
P  M  T  S  A  M  R  R  B  Y  F
E  E  Y  X  L  C  E  E  W  J  A
T  M  A  N  L  D  V  W  R  A  S
E  O  R  V  I  U  N  O  L  N  O
R  A  J  P  V  B  X  P  R  E  R
W  L  S  Q  M  A  S  V  R  E  C
```

VILLAIN	SPIDER-MAN	SWING
POWER	MARY JANE	BUILDING
MASK	CRIME	PETER

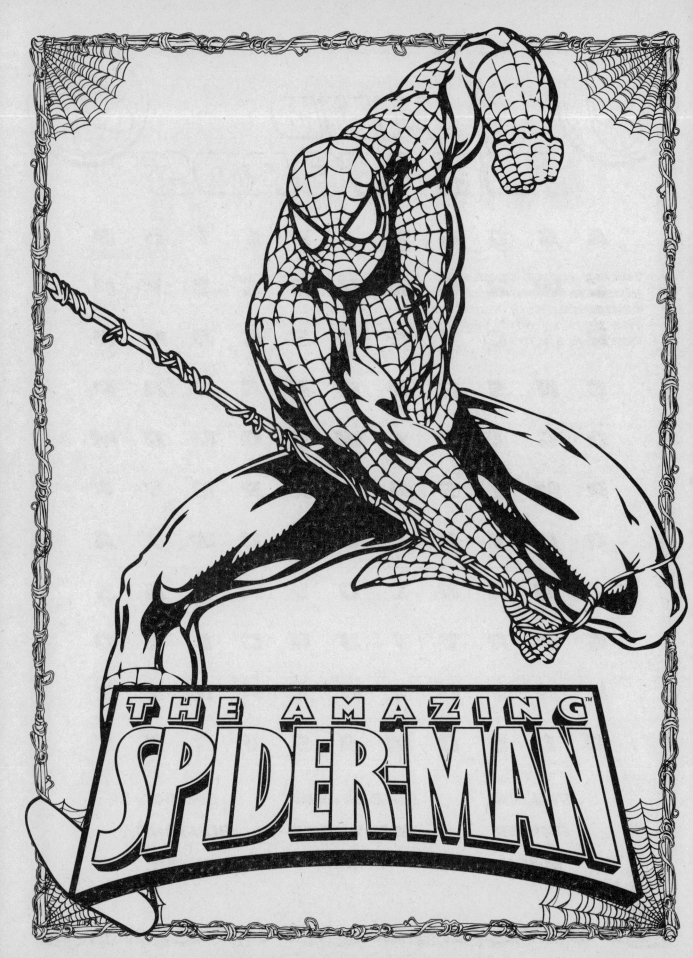

DOCTOR OCTOPUS

SQUARES

Taking turns, connect a line from one pair of glasses to another. Whoever makes the line that completes a box puts their initials inside the box. The person with the most squares at the end of the game wins!

EXAMPLE:

SPIDER-SENSE

PUZZLE

Using the list below, unscramble the letters of the words.
Fill in the numbered letters in the spaces at the bottom to create a new word!

WORD LIST

VULTURE	STRENGTH	SPIDER
CARNAGE	RHINO	

NOIHR ___ ___ ___ ___ ___
8.   9.

RUTEVLU ___ ___ ___ ___ ___ ___ ___
2.   5.

ERGNTTHS ___ ___ ___ ___ ___ ___ ___ ___
1.   6.

EIDRPS ___ ___ ___ ___ ___ ___
3.   7.

NARAGEC ___ ___ ___ ___ ___ ___ ___
4.

1.	2.	3.	4.	5.	6.	7.	8.	9.

Draw the

GREEN GOBLIN

Using the grid as a guide, draw a picture of the Green Goblin in the box below.

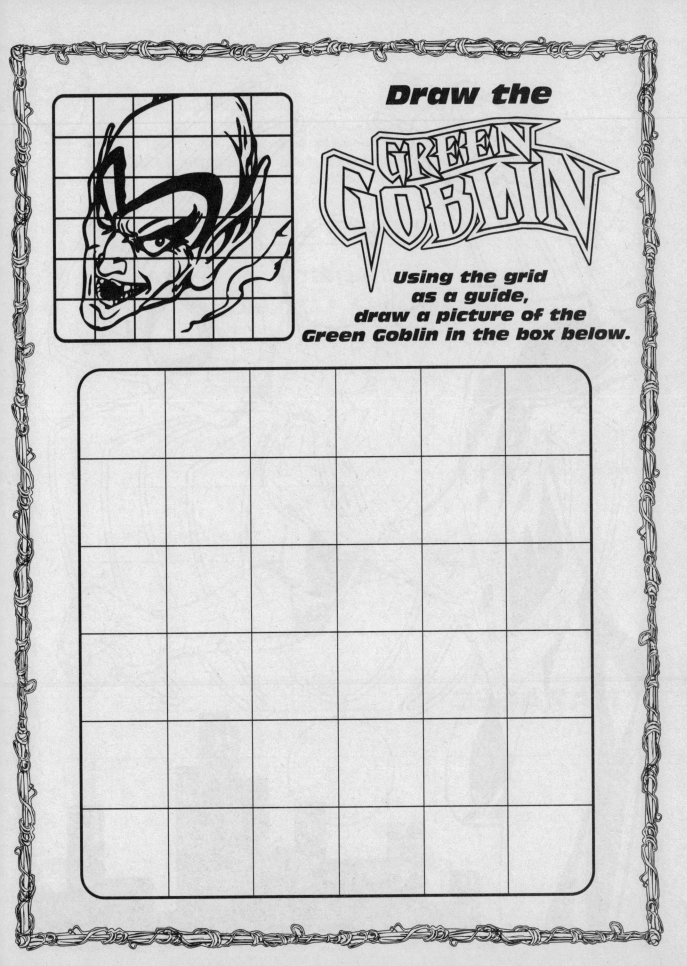

TIC-TAC-TOE

USE THESE SPACES TO CHALLENGE YOUR FAMILY AND FRIENDS!

SPIDEY MAZE

Help M.J. get through the maze and reach Spider-Man!

START

FINISH

VENOM

PUZZLE

Have a parent or care-giver cut out the puzzle pieces on the dotted lines.

Mix up the pieces, and put the picture back together!

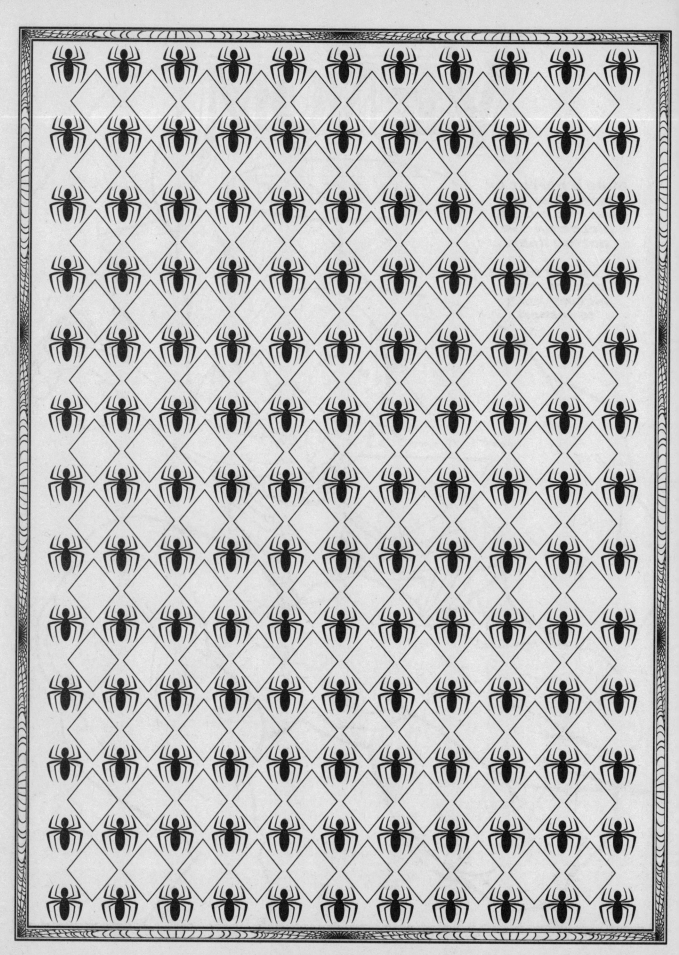

WHICH AUNT MAY IS
DIFFERENT?

One AUNT MAY below is an imposter. Can you find the one that is different from the others?

1.

2.

3.

4.

Crack the Code!

Use the code below to fill in the blanks and reveal the secret words!

___ ___ ___ ___ ___ ___   ___ ___ ___ ___
17. 8. 22. 2. 24. 9.   1. 22. 10. 24.

___ ___ ___ ___ ___ ___ ___ ___
17. 10. 9. 24. 7. 23. 10. 4.

___ ___ ___ ___ ___ ___ ___ ___ ___ ___ ___ ___ ___
17. 8. 22. 2. 24. 9. 20. 26. 7. 17. 15. 24. 1.

___ ___ ___ ___ ___   ___ ___ ___
1. 6. 26. 25. 21.   25. 26. 10.

___ ___ ___ ___ ___ ___ ___
11. 16. 6. 10. 16. 9. 24.

1.	2.	3.	4.	5.	6.	7.	8.	9.	10.	11.
B	D	F	H	J	L	N	P	R	T	V

12.	13.	14.	15.	16.	17.	18.	19.	20.	21.	22.
X	Z	Y	W	U	S	Q	O	M	K	I

23.	24.	25.	26.
G	E	C	A

Secret Message!

Cross out the words DOCTOR OCTOPUS every time you see them in the box. When you reach a letter that does not belong, write it in the circles below to spell the secret words!

DOCTOROCTOPUSODOCT
OROCTOPUSTDOCTOROC
TOPUSTDOCTOROCTOPUS
ODOCTOROCTOPUSODOCT
OROCTOPUSCDOCTOROC
TOPUSTDOCTOROCTOPUS
ADOCTOROCTOPUSVDOCT
OROCTOPUSIDOCTOROCT
OPUSUDOCTOROCTOPUSS

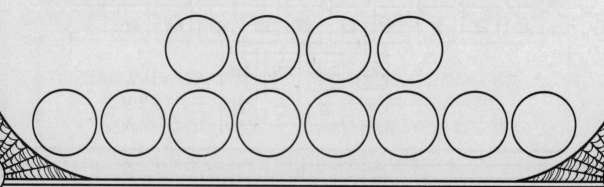

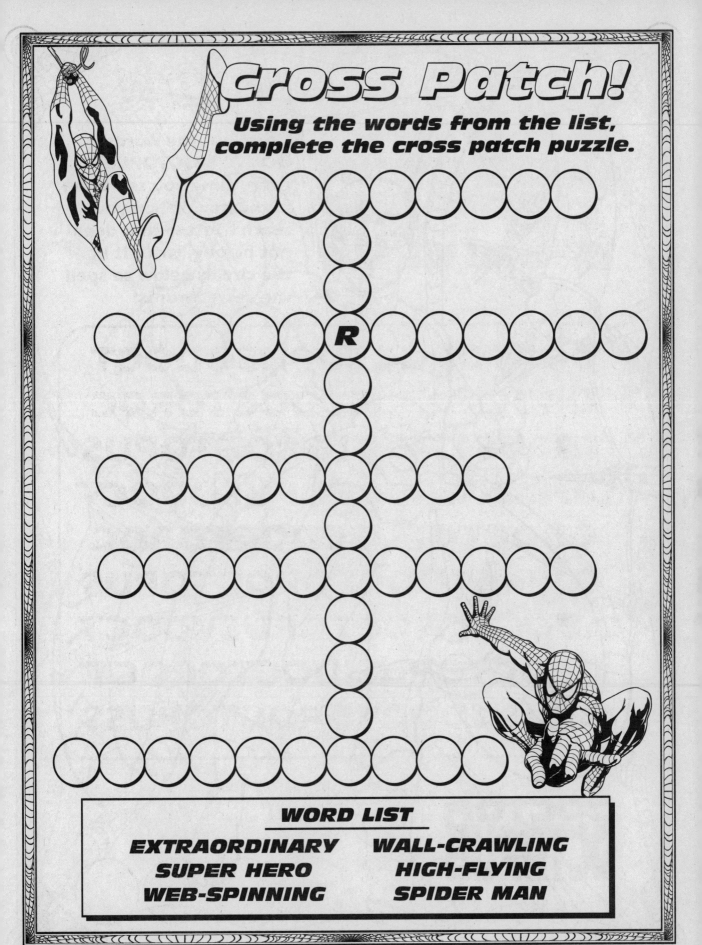

Cross Patch!

Using the words from the list, complete the cross patch puzzle.

R

WORD LIST

EXTRAORDINARY	**WALL-CRAWLING**
SUPER HERO	**HIGH-FLYING**
WEB-SPINNING	**SPIDER MAN**

DOCTOR OCTOPUS

Which 2 are EXACTLY the SAME?

Look at the four pictures. Two of them are exactly alike.
Can you find them?

1.

2.

3.

4.

Answers: Numbers 2 and 3.

FIND THE WORDS

```
S  T  R  E  N  G  T  H  O  P  E
A  V  A  S  P  R  C  H  E  A  K
O  L  U  F  R  E  W  O  P  R  I
R  A  P  V  A  C  H  B  Q  K  L
E  J  K  R  D  C  B  G  N  E  R
H  Z  A  C  I  R  Y  O  W  R  E
R  U  E  M  A  K  V  B  S  J  D
E  A  Q  W  T  V  I  L  R  C  I
P  X  S  P  I  N  N  I  N  G  P
U  U  I  O  O  R  T  N  Z  A  S
S  R  H  G  N  I  L  W  A  R  C
```

HOB GOBLIN	SPINNING	CRAWLING
POWERFUL	SPIDER-LIKE	SUPER HERO
RADIATION	PARKER	STRENGTH

Follow the Path

Using the letters in order from the word
VENOM
follow the correct path to find your way through the maze!

Word Scramble

Using the words from the list, unscramble the letters to correctly spell the names and words!

RHEERPUOS _____

NEGRTTHS _____

REWDIEPBS _____

KCCALABT _____

ROADRITNAXRYE _____

RBEIDTEIPS _____

WORD LIST

SPIDER BITE	**BLACK CAT**
STRENGTH	**EXTRAORDINARY**
SPIDER WEB	**SUPER HERO**

SPIDER-SQUARES

Taking turns, connect a line from one face to another. Whoever makes the line that completes a box puts their initials inside the box. The person with the most squares at the end of the game wins!

EXAMPLE:

Which Piece is
MISSING?

Only one of the puzzle pieces below will fit. Can you find the missing piece and complete the puzzle?

A.

B.

C.

TIC-TAC-TOE

USE THESE SPACES TO CHALLENGE YOUR FAMILY AND FRIENDS!

WHICH SPIDER-MAN IS
DIFFERENT?

One SPIDER-MAN below is an imposter. Can you find the one that is different from the others?

1.

2.

3.

4.

WHO is WHO?

Match the pictures of the villains by writing the correct letter below each close-up!

 **A.**

 **B.**

 **C.**

 **D.**

 **1.**

 **2.**

 **3.**

 **4.**

 **5.**

 **6.**

 **7.**

 **8.**

RHINO

SPIDEY MAZE

Help the Amazing Spider-Man get through the maze and capture Sandman!

START

FINISH

FIND THE WORDS

```
R  S  C  I  T  E  L  H  T  A  Y
F  Q  T  B  A  O  E  M  Z  I  T
E  B  U  R  G  L  E  R  M  J  I
L  W  T  L  E  C  N  R  Q  R  L
I  Q  A  P  U  N  O  S  A  O  I
C  Y  C  Y  M  F  G  O  L  A  G
I  S  K  X  S  I  R  T  E  K  A
A  M  C  N  X  A  L  E  H  L  C
Z  X  A  C  P  C  L  A  W  S  Z
P  R  L  Q  G  M  K  S  D  O  A
T  X  B  V  W  Z  R  Y  M  T  P
```

BLACK CAT   **AGILITY**   **BURGLER**

FELICIA   **STRENGTH**   **TRANSFORM**

POWERFUL   **CLAWS**   **ATHLETIC**

TIC-TAC-TOE

USE THESE SPACES TO CHALLENGE YOUR FAMILY AND FRIENDS!

SPIDER-SENSE
PUZZLE

Using the list below, unscramble the letters of the words.
Fill in the numbered letters in the spaces at the bottom to create a new word!

WORD LIST

AMAZING   SPIDER WEB   PROTECTOR

STRENGTH   SPIDER BITE

ENGRTTHS __ __ __ __ __ __ __ __
                    10.   5.

REDBIITPES __ __ __ __ __ __ __ __ __
                          3.   9.

ECTTOORRP __ __ __ __ __ __ __ __ __
                    6.   7.   2.

REDWIEPBS __ __ __ __ __ __ __ __ __
                                              8.

ZAMIANG __ __ __ __ __ __ __
                    4.   1.

1.	2.	3.	4.	5.	6.	7.	8.	9.	10.

FIND THE WORDS

```
Z S G E N I U S V R E
L T J G X C R U E P V
P C E Z Q E O P K B I
S R X N C G H O V E L
U I T S T V W T N M M
I M R Q C A J C K Y I
V I Y R O T C O D K N
A N A M R K P L U Q D
T A Z Q E L Z S E U O
C L S E G N O R T S P
O Q T K I T E R C Y R
```

DOCTOR	TENTACLES	STRONG
OCTOPUS	ENEMY	EVIL MIND
OCTAVIUS	GENIUS	CRIMINAL

Finish the Picture!
Spider-Man is fighting a dangerous battle!
Draw your own version of a villain.

BLACK CAT PUZZLE

Have a parent or care-giver cut out the puzzle pieces on the dotted lines.

Mix up the pieces and put the picture back together!

GOBLIN SQUARES

Taking turns, connect a line from one pumpkin to another. Whoever makes the line that completes a box puts their initials inside the box. The person with the most squares at the end of the game wins!

EXAMPLE:

A

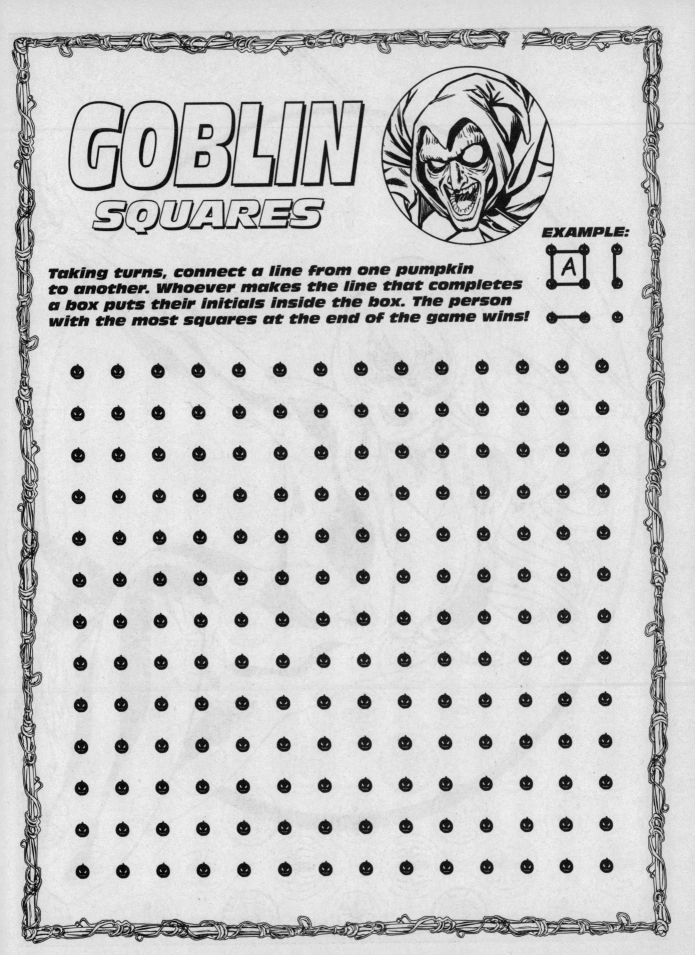

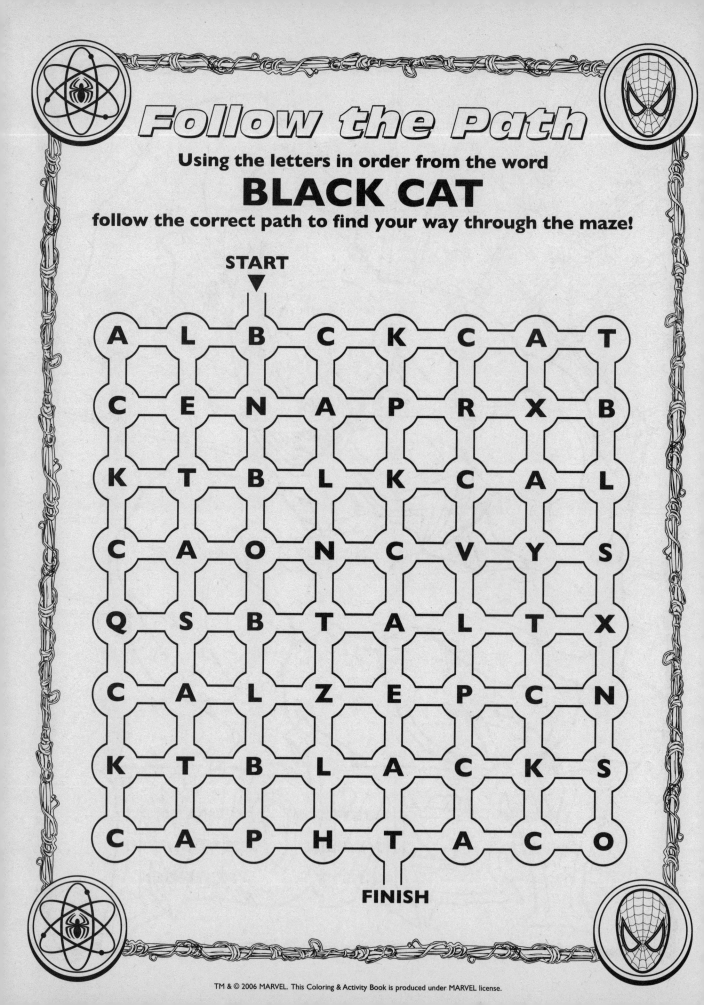

Follow the Path

Using the letters in order from the word

BLACK CAT

follow the correct path to find your way through the maze!

START ▼

A	L	B	C	K	C	A	T
C	E	N	A	P	R	X	B
K	T	B	L	K	C	A	L
C	A	O	N	C	V	Y	S
Q	S	B	T	A	L	T	X
C	A	L	Z	E	P	C	N
K	T	B	L	A	C	K	S
C	A	P	H	T	A	C	O

FINISH

FIND THE WORDS

```
S D R W C O N N E R S
U T V D R A Z I L E P
J R N O P E T Y U P I
T A M E L Q B W F T S
E N C W M E C O R I O
W S A J G I R F E L A
M F C M S M R I W E B
Z O G H U C H E O L T
B R T L J H L T P O P
X M A Q V I N G Y X R
E B R A G I L I T Y E
```

LIZARD	TRANSFORM	POWERFUL
CONNERS	INHUMAN	EXPERIMENT
REPTILE	AGILITY	FORMULA

WHO is WHO?

Match the pictures of the faces by writing the correct letter below each close-up!

A.

B.

C.

D.

1.

2.

3.

4.

5.

6.

7.

8.

TIC-TAC-TOE

USE THESE SPACES TO CHALLENGE YOUR FAMILY AND FRIENDS!

ELECTRO SQUARES

EXAMPLE:

Taking turns, connect a line from one lightning bolt to another. Whoever makes the line that completes a box puts their initials inside the box. The person with the most squares at the end of the game wins!

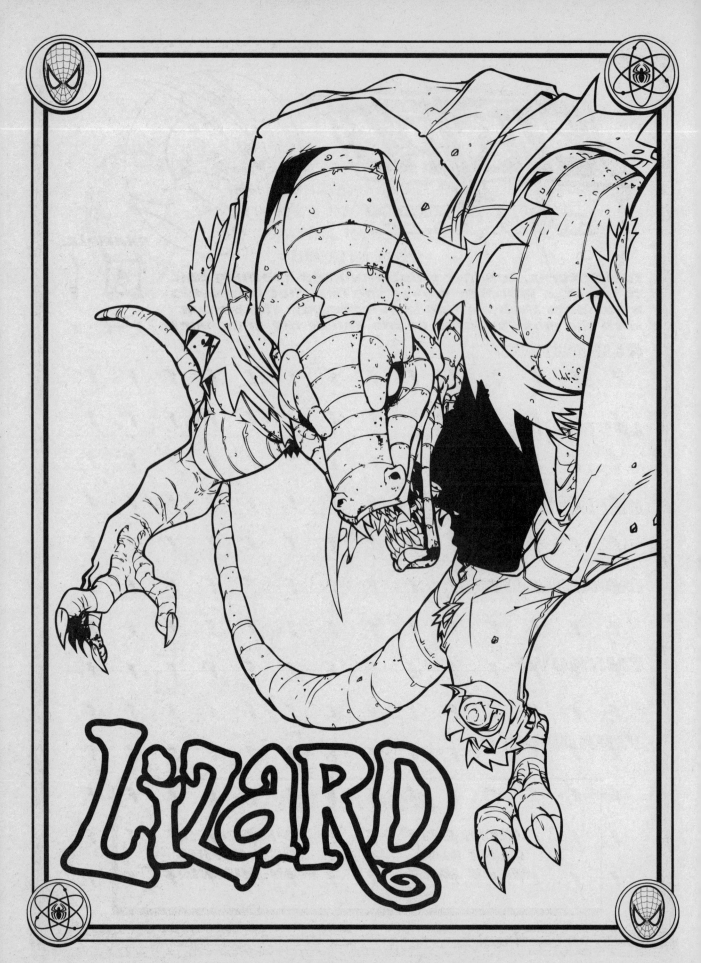

Word Scramble

Using the words from the list, unscramble the letters to correctly spell the names and words!

RLEIDKIESP _____

LFYHGIINGH _____

EBLECNNU _____

INPNSIBNEGW _____

TMNAUYA _____

YJRAANME _____

WORD LIST

UNCLE BEN	SPIDER-LIKE
AUNT MAY	HIGH-FLYING
MARY JANE	WEB-SPINNING

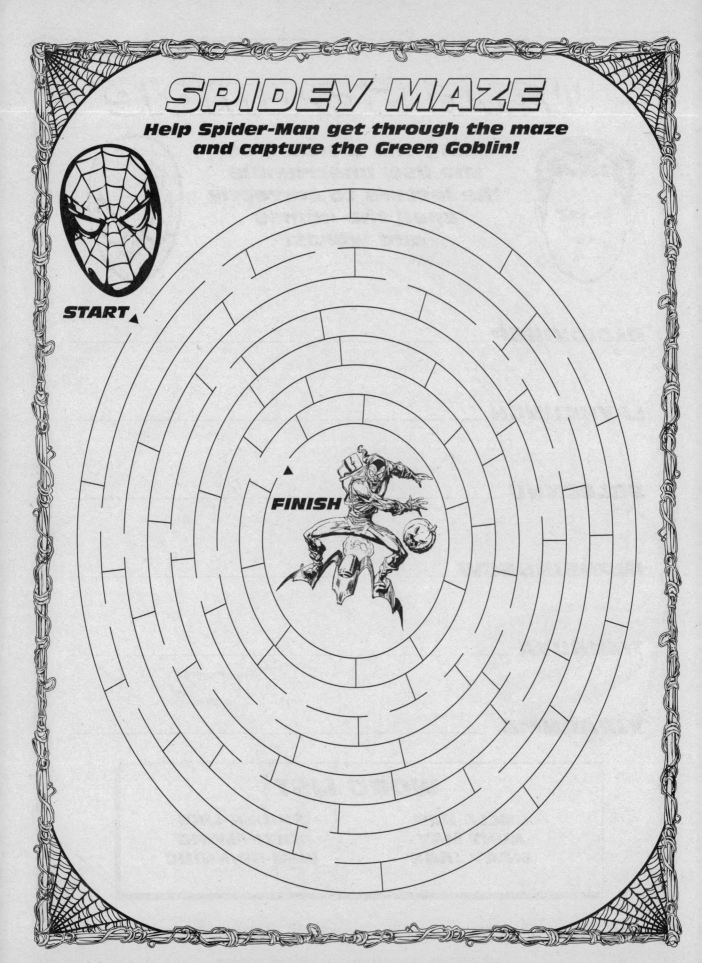

Secret Message!

Cross out the words VENOM every time you see them in the box. When you reach a letter that does not belong, write it in the circles below to spell the secret words!

VENOMEVENOMDVENOM
VENOMVENOMDVENOM
VENOMIVENOMVENOME
VENOMVENOMBVENOM
VENOMRVENOMVENOM
VENOMVENOMOVENOM
VENOMCVENOMVENOM
VENOMVENOMVENOM
VENOMVENOMKVENOM

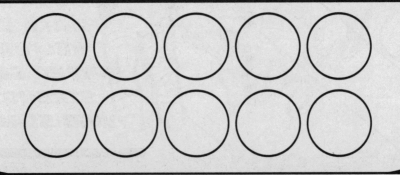

Cross Patch!

Using the words from the list, complete the cross patch puzzle.

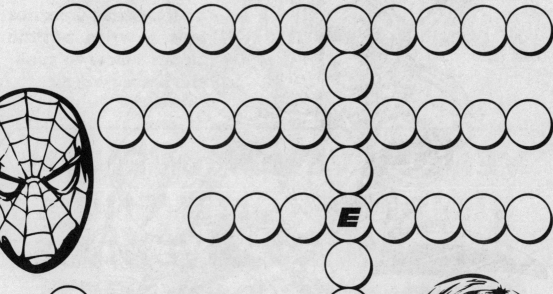

WHICH DOCTOR OCTOPUS IS
DIFFERENT?

One DOCTOR OCTOPUS below is an imposter. Can you find the one that is different from the others?

1.

2.

3.

4.

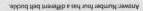

Answer: Number four has a different belt buckle.

Finish the Picture!

Finish drawing a city below Spider-Man as he races to fight crime!

FIND THE WORDS

```
M K U R E T S I N I S
J E T H C I T R W H B
L I N V E N T O R X M
Y S A G E G N E V E R
O A I R I W T Q U S V
T V L C M N B L L D I
H P L A B O E C T R L
G A I R C M T E U Y L
I O R E W O P N R B A
L P B V C W K U E V I
F R M R U R C L B I N
```

VULTURE	SINISTER	REVENGE
ENGINEER	POWER	BRILLIANT
INVENTOR	FLIGHT	VILLAIN

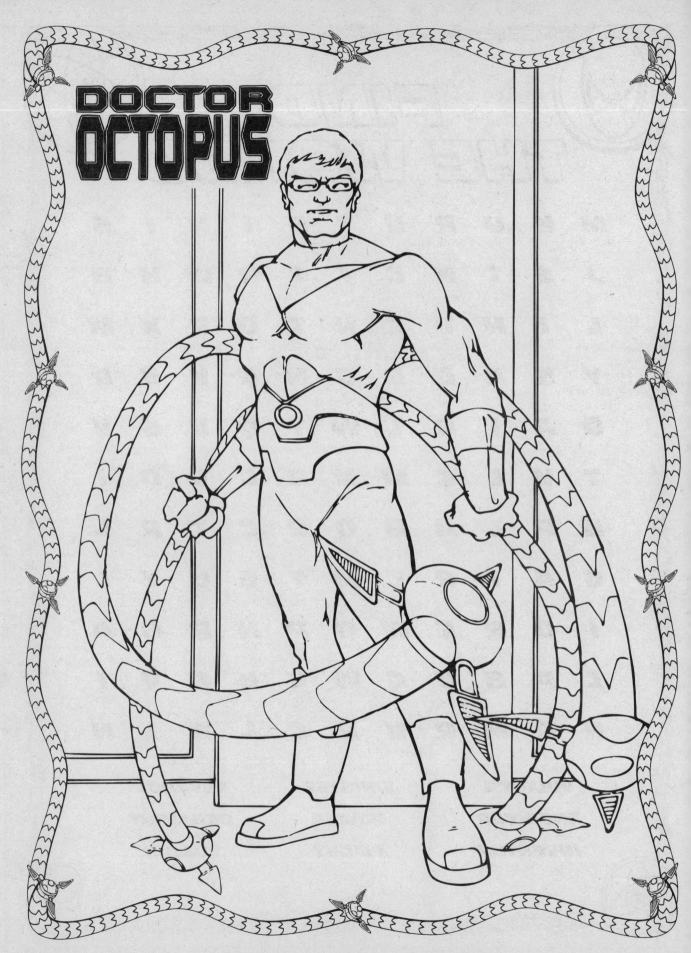

DOCTOR
OCTOPUS

OUR WORLD IN COLOUR
HONG KONG

OUR WORLD IN COLOUR HONGKONG

Photography by Airphoto International,
China Guides Series, Alain Evrard, Neil Farrin,
Greg Girard, Pat Lam, Joan Law,
Leong Ka Tai, Francis Li, Keith Macgregor,
James Montgomery, Lincoln Potter,
C.T.H. Smith, Carolyn Watts,
Steve Weinrebe, Angela Wong,
Wong Chun Wai, Jacky Yip and
Vincent Yu

Text and captions by Amanda Agee

The Guidebook Company Limited

Distributors
Australia and New Zealand: The Book Company, 100 Old Pittwater Road, Brookvale, NSW 2100, Australia.

Canada: Prentice Hall Canada, 1870 Birchmount Road, Scarborough, Ontario MIP 257, Canada.

Hong Kong: China Guides Distribution Services Ltd., 14 Ground Floor, Lower Kai Yuen Lane, North Point, Hong Kong.

India and Nepal: UBS Publishers' Distributors Ltd., 5 Ansari Road, Post Box 7015, New Delhi 110 002, India.

Singapore and Malaysia: MPH Distributors (S) PTE Ltd., 601 Sims Drive, No. 03/07-21, Pan-I Complex, Singapore 1438.

UK: Springfield Books Limited, Springfield House, Norman Road, Dendy Dale, Huddersfield HD8 8TH, West Yorkshire, England.

USA: Publishers Group West Inc., 4065 Hollis, Emeryville, CA 94608, USA.

Photography by Airphoto International (6–7, 12–13, 17 centre, 24–25 top/bottom right, 26, 27, 28–29, 30, 31, 32, 49, 60–61, 66 top, 67); China Guides Series (39 bottom right, 63 second from top left); Alain Evrard, The Stock House (48); Neil Farrin, Images (16 top, 17 top, 24 bottom left, 33, 38, 72); Greg Girard (5, 17 Bottom, 22, 23 left three, 36, 39 top right, 42 top, 43 left three, 51, 73, 75 centre/bottom); Pat Lam (18 bottom, 44 all four, 45); Joan Law (10–11, 19 top/bottom, 20 all three, 21, 35 centre left, 39 bottom left, 46 top/bottom, 47, 50, 52, 54, 58 all, 59, 60–61 bottom three, 63 right, 64, 69, 71, 77); Leong Ka Tai (43 right); Francis Li, The Stock House (35 top left); C.T.H. Smith, Images (16 bottom, 66 bottom); Carolyn Watts (70); Steve Weinrebe, The Stock House (35 bottom left); Wong Chun Wai (68, 78–79); Angela Wong (63 bottom left); Jacky Yip, China Photo Library (8–9, 41, 53, 55, 56, 63 top left, 75 top)

	2	
1	3	4
5		6
		7

Page 74:

Joan Law 1, 2, 4, 5, 6;
James Montgomery 7;
Vincent Yu 3.

Text and captions by Amanda Agee
Edited by Nick Wallwork
Series Editor: Rose Borton
Photo Editor: Caroline Robertson
Original designed by Joan Law Design & Photography
Artwork by Aubrey Tse, Au Yeung Chui Kwai

Printed in Hong Kong

ISBN 962-217-112–5

Title spread
As the sun drops slowly behind Hong Kong's many outlying islands, a rare stillness descends over the harbour. During the day, these same waters churn with the traffic of thousands of vessels from all over the world.

Right
While the activity in some parts of the territory ebbs away with the setting sun, Hong Kong's night markets are just getting started. Hawkers begin setting up shop around seven in the evening offering everything from food to pirated cassettes or the latest in badly made copies of designer sportswear. Some of the larger night markets are Temple Street Market near Jordan, and the 'Poor Man's Nightclub' near the Macau Ferry Pier.

Pages 6-7
The urban landscape of Hong Kong Island and the Kowloon Peninsula gives little evidence of the colony's almost wholly barren state when it was founded nearly 150 years ago. Business complexes such as Exchange Square and Jardine House (centre) line the harbour, with the equally imposing residential towers of the Mid-levels creeping up the mountains behind.

Pages 8-9
East meets West in no uncertain terms during the Dragon Boat Festival. Junks embellished with flags and dragon heads carry on a centuries-old tradition while the high-tech heights of Tsimshatsui in the background are a vigorous reminder of the present.

Pages 10-11
Opera to placate marauding ghosts and charm the hearts of humans. Members of one of Hong Kong's two main fishing tribes, the Hoklo, perform during the Cheung Chau Bun Festival.

Pages 12-13
Tradition continues in Hong Kong in ways other than just festivals. Ancient farming methods are practised in fish ponds such as these near Yuen Long in the New Territories. Different species of carp are the main products with about 5,700 tonnes harvested annually.